DUDLEY SCHOOLS
LIBRARY SERVICE

D0310220

Schools Library and Information Service

S00000612550

Life cycle of a BROAD BEAN

Angela Royston

Heinemann LIBRARY

First published in Great Britain by Heinemann Library
Halley Court, Jordan Hill, Oxford OX2 8EJ
a division of Reed Educational and Professional Publishing Ltd

Heinemann is a registered trademark of Reed Educational and Professional Publishing Limited.

OXFORD   MELBOURNE   AUCKLAND
IBADAN   BLANTYRE   JOHANNESBURG   GABORONE
PORTSMOUTH NH   CHICAGO

© Reed Educational and Professional Publishing Ltd 2000
The moral right of the proprietor has been asserted.

All rights reserved. No part of this publication may be reproduced, stored in a retrieval system, or transmitted in any form or by any means, electronic, mechanical, photocopying, recording, or otherwise without either the prior written permission of the Publishers or a licence permitting restricted copying in the United Kingdom issued by the Copyright Licensing Agency Ltd, 90 Tottenham Court Road, London W1P 0LP.

Designed by Celia Floyd
Illustrations by Alan Fraser
Originated by Dot Gradations, UK
Printed in Hong Kong/China

04 03 02 01 00
10 9 8 7 6 5 4 3 2 1

ISBN 0 431 08402 5

DUDLEY PUBLIC LIBRARIES
L 44395
612550   SCH
JY635

British Library Cataloguing in Publication Data

Royston, Angela
   Life cycle of a broad bean. – (Take-off!)
   1.Fava bean – Life cycles- Juvenile literature
   I.Title II.Broad Bean
   583.7'4

Acknowledgements
The Publisher would like to thank the following for permission to reproduce photographs:
A–Z Botanical Collection Ltd/Moira C Smith p10; Bruce Coleman Ltd/Adrian Davies p23; Chris Honeywell pp17, 18; Harry Smith Collection pp6, 14, 20, 21, 22, 26/27; Heather Angel p13; OSF/G A Maclean p19; OSF/G I Bernard pp7, 8, 9; OSF/J A L Cooke p12; The Garden Picture Library/David Askham p25; The Garden Picture Library/Mayer Le Scanff p5; The Garden Picture/Michael Howes pp11, 24; Roger Scruton p4; Trevor Clifford p15.
Cover photograph: Harry Smith Collection

Our thanks to Sue Graves for her advice and expertise in the preparation of this book.

Every effort has been made to contact copyright holders of any material reproduced in this book. Any omissions will be rectified in subsequent printings if notice is given to the Publisher.

For more information about Heinemann Library books, or to order, please telephone +44(0)1865 888066, or send a fax to +44(0)1865 314091. You can visit our website at www.heinemann.co.uk

Any words appearing in bold, **like this**, are explained in the Glossary.

Contents

What is a bean?

black-eyed beans

red kidney beans

broad beans

Here are some black-eyed beans, red kidney beans and broad beans.

A bean is a **seed**. It grows in a **pod** on a tall, climbing plant. Many people like to eat beans. There are many types to choose from and they are all different shapes and sizes.

1 day

1 week

2 weeks

6 weeks

These are broad beans and broad bean pods.

The beans in this picture are called broad beans. In this book you will find out what happens to a broad bean which is planted in spring.

12 weeks

14 weeks

20 weeks

1–7 days

The bean seeds need space to grow.

The bean **seed** is planted in the soil with other bean seeds. The seeds are not planted too close together so each seed has space to grow. The soil is watered and the beans begin to grow.

1 day

1 week

2 weeks

6 weeks

A root has 2 jobs to do. It holds the plant into the ground and it takes water and **minerals** out of the soil to help the plant grow.

seed coat

root

A root grows first.

The first part of the plant to grow from the seed is the **root**. The root pushes out through the seed coat and grows down into the soil. It grows longer and longer.

12 weeks

14 weeks

20 weeks

2–3 weeks

The next part of the plant to grow is the **shoot**. The bent **stem** pushes upwards through the soil. At the end of the stem there are tiny leaves.

stem

The shoot grows next.

1 day

1 week

2 weeks

6 weeks

The shoot pushes right up through the soil. Then the stem straightens. The leaves at the top of the stem open out. More **roots** are growing all the time.

roots

The stem straightens when it has pushed right through the soil.

12 weeks

14 weeks

20 weeks

3–10 weeks

As soon as the leaves grow, they start to make food for the plant.

Once the leaves open out, they turn dark green in the light. The leaves make food for the plant so that it can grow. The leaves use sunlight, air and water to make food for the plant.

| 1 day | 1 week | 2 weeks | 6 weeks |

The plant grows more quickly and starts to make flowers.

Water and **minerals** from the soil pass through the **roots** and up the **stem** to the leaves. The bean plant grows quickly. Flower **buds** form and start to open out into flowers.

12 weeks

14 weeks

20 weeks

11 weeks

These blackfly are attacking the leaf of the plant.

Blackfly can attack bean plants. They lay their eggs under the leaves. These blackfly have **hatched** out of the eggs. Now they are eating the leaves.

1 day   1 week   2 weeks   6 weeks

Blackfly are small insects that feed on the liquid inside a plant.

Ladybirds save plants by eating the blackfly.

If a plant's leaves become too damaged, they cannot make food for the plant and it will die. Blackfly can kill a plant. Ladybirds eat lots of blackfly and help to save the plant.

12 weeks

14 weeks

20 weeks

12 weeks

Broad bean plants make clusters of flowers.

The broad bean plant makes thick **clusters** of flowers at the bottom of the leaves. These flowers have black and white petals.

1 day   1 week   2 weeks   6 weeks

There are grains of pollen and nectar in the middle of this flower.

Tiny grains of **pollen** and a sweet juice called **nectar** are found in the middle of each flower. Insects, such as bees, come to each flower to drink the nectar.

Bees make honey from nectar.

12 weeks

14 weeks

20 weeks

12 weeks

This bee has grains of pollen stuck to it.

pollen

The bee crawls right into the flower to reach the **nectar**. As it sips the nectar, grains of **pollen** stick to its hairy legs and body. Can you see the pollen sticking to this bee?

1 day

1 week

2 weeks

6 weeks

When a bee takes pollen from one flower to another, it is called pollination.

Grains of pollen from another flower rub off the bee inside this flower.

While the bee is inside this flower, some pollen from another flower rubs off its body. This other pollen joins a **pod** of **seeds**.

12 weeks

14 weeks

20 weeks

12–14 weeks

The flower is no longer needed so it wilts and dies.

When a **seed** inside the **pod** joins with a grain of **pollen** from another flower, it becomes a new bean. The flower dies and the beans swell.

1 day

1 week

2 weeks

6 weeks

pod

The beans are protected inside these pods.

The beans grow inside the pods. Pods are thick, tough shells that protect the growing bean. As the beans grow, the pod grows longer and heavier.

12 weeks

14 weeks

20 weeks

14 weeks

This plant has grown many pods.

By 14 weeks the plants are covered with **pods**. Look how many pods are growing on this plant. How many pods can you see?

1 day

1 week

2 weeks

6 weeks

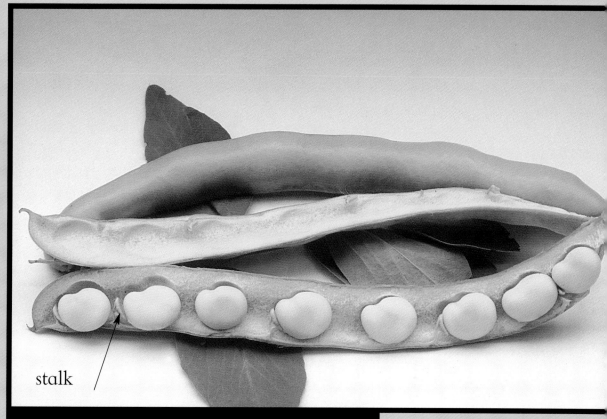

stalk

Each bean is joined to the pod by a stalk.

The inside of a pod is soft and damp. It is damp because the beans must not dry out. Each bean is joined to the pod by a very short **stalk**. The stalk brings food and water to the bean.

12 weeks

14 weeks

20 weeks

20 weeks

At about 20 weeks, the beans are fully grown. The **pods** begin to turn black. Now the plant has done its job. Its leaves begin to wilt and die.

These pods are starting to turn black because the beans are fully grown.

1 day

1 week

2 weeks

6 weeks

This field mouse likes to eat beans.

When the beans are fully grown, some of the
pods fall to the ground. Small animals, like this
field mouse, like to eat beans. When a field
mouse finds a pod which has split open, it
quickly eats up the beans.

12 weeks

14 weeks

20 weeks

20–24 weeks

Beans are usually picked between 20 and 24 weeks.

The best time to pick beans is just before they are fully grown. They are more juicy to eat then. In autumn, the whole plant withers and dies.

1 day   1 week   2 weeks   6 weeks

These beans have been saved to be planted next spring.

Not all of the beans are eaten. Some are saved.
They are left to dry and go hard and brown.
These are the new **seeds** which will be planted
next spring. They will grow into new plants
which will make more broad beans.

12 weeks

14 weeks

20 weeks

A field of beans

Farmers plant huge fields of beans like this.

Some people like to grow just a few bean plants in their gardens. Farmers plant huge fields of beans like this one. The **pods** are picked and sent to factories. In the factories, the beans are frozen or put into tins.

Once all the pods have been picked, the farmer cuts up the plants and covers them with soil. Slowly, the plants rot and break up. They become part of the soil. The rotting plants are good for the soil.

Life cycle

1 day

1 week

2 weeks

6 weeks

12 weeks

14 weeks

20 weeks

Fact file

In just four months a broad bean grows from a seed to a plant as tall as an adult person.

The bean that Jack planted in *Jack and the Beanstalk* was a broad bean.

One broad bean plant can produce over 300 beans.

In Ancient Greece and Rome, rich people would not eat broad beans because they thought they would damage their eyesight.

Glossary

bud   a flower before it opens

cluster   group

hatch   to be born out of an egg

minerals   chemicals that plants need to stay healthy

nectar   a sweet, sugary juice in the centre of a flower

pod   a tough, thick shell that surrounds the beans

pollen   fine yellow dust made in the centre of a flower

root   part of a plant under the ground which takes in water from the soil

seed   the fruit of a plant which can grow into a new plant

shoot   the first stem and leaves of a new plant

stalk   the part of a plant that supports it. Also called a stem

stem   the part of a plant that supports the leaves, flowers and fruit of a plant

Index